The Mystery Fancier

Wildside Press / 301-762-1305

L6010309

Title Information:

978-1-4344-3633-7

The Mystery Fancier, Vol. 6, No. 5

Volume 6, Number 5
September/October 1982

The Mystery Fancier

Volume 6, Number 5
September/October 1982

TABLE OF CONTENTS

The Mystery Fancier
(USPS:428-590)
is edited and published bi-monthly by
Guy M. Townsend
1711 Clifty Drive
Madison, IN 47250

SUBSCRIPTION RATES: Domestic second class mail, $12.00 per year (6 issues); overseas surface mail, $12.00; overseas airmail, $18.00. Overseas subscribers please pay in international money order, check drawn on U.S. bank, or currency; no checks drawn on foreign banks, please.
Single copy price: $2.50

Second class postage paid at Madison, Indiana.

WILDSIDE PRESS

An Index to TMF Volumes I - V
(Including the Preview Issue)
Compiled by Charles K. Cook

Adey,Bob
  L:V.C.Clinton-Baddeley;H.Keeler;Locked room mys-
    teries   1/3/51
  L:Some recommended reading;H.F.Wiber-Wood;Shafer's
    WITNESSED MURDER;Obscure British paperbacks   2/3/73
  L:Hon Con;R.Winsor;Holmes on the BBC;Colin Watson
    Flaxborough Chronicles on the BBC   2/4/57
  L:"Big Four";Missing art objects stories;Queen au-
    thorship;Query about P.Godfrey;The Meyersons   3/1/59
  L:Locked room bibliography;Lost Abercrombie Lewker
    stories;Author using same detective under
    different pennames   3/3/60
  L:Several new publications in England including
    MISS MARPLE'S SIX FINAL CASES   3/5/46
  L:P.Lovesey's books on TV in England;Rumpole;Enigma
    Files of C.Sparks   4/3/48
  L:G.Higgin's books;Sherlockian Blocks;Breen's book;
    Original Sgt.Cribb stories for British TV   5/3/43
  L:W.C.Gault;T.B.Dewey;20th CC&MW;Academic writing;
    TV mysteries;TV spin-off books   5/4/44
  L:Favorite articles;Publisher errors   5/5/47
  L:Gillespie's THE CROSSWORD MYSTERY;D.Gordon's
    ROSE MEDALLION   5/6/53
  R:BRIGHTLIGHT(T.Bernard)   4/3/42
  R:CROSS THAT PALM WHEN I COME TO IT(A.Southcott)   5/2/38
  R:DEATH DROP(B.M.Gill)   5/4/34
  R:HERO BY PROXY(D.Teilhet)   5/3/40
  R:HIS MASTER'S VOICE(I.Low)   5/3/40
  R:LOOKING FOR RACHEL WALLACE(R.B.Parker)   5/5/36
  R:A MAN CALLED SCAVENER(P.Van Greenaway)   5/4/33
  R:THE MYSTERY GUILD ANTHOLOGY   5/2/38
  R:THE PENNY MURDERS(L.Black)   5/5/37
  R:THE SECOND DEADLY SIN(L.Sanders)   5/4/33
  R:SERGEANT VERITY AND THE BLOOD ROYAL(F.Selwyn)   3/6/48
  R:THE TURN UP(A.Stewart)   5/2/38
  R:WHO IS TEDDY VILLANOVA?(T.Berger)   5/5/36
  R:YOU NICE BASTARD(G.F.Newman)   2/2/37
  TWO FROM THE TELLY(SAPPHIRE AND STEEL,THE
    PROFESSIONALS)   5/6/19
AGATHA CHRISTIE IS STILL ALIVE AND WELL(A.Kabatchnik)   2/6/9

6

```
R:LIGNY'S LAKES(S.H.Courtier)                            5/5/42
R:THE LUCK RUNS OUT(C.MacLeod)                           5/5/37
R:MURDER TRAPP(E.Franklin)                               5/5/42
R:MY FOE OUTSTRETCH'D BENEATH THE TREE
  (V.C.Clinton-Baddeley)                                 5/5/37
R:ROASTED EGGS(D.Clark)                                  5/4/36
R:SHORT CIRCUIT(L.Oriol)                                 5/5/39
R:TELL YOU WHAT I'LL DO(H.Cecil)                         5/5/38
R:THE THREE WORLDS OF JOHNNY HANDSOME(J.Godey)           5/5/43
THE (VERY TEMPORARY)RETURN OF SKULL-FACE                 2/2/21
Broecker,Jay    L:Collections;Queries about lists and
  authors                                                2/3/57
Broset,Myrtis
  L:Fanzine following;Mynah bird                         1/2/48
  L:Purpose of TMF;Mystery fans vs mystery
    collectors                                           1/6/58
  L:Violent action vs ratiocination;Mystery readers  2/1/59
  L:Art work;Women and mysteries;Reviewers            2/2/42
  L:Christie in THE SATURDAY EVENING POST;Keating's
    AGATHA CHRISTIE.FIRST LADY OF CRIME                  2/2/59
  L:Reviewing;Criticism of reviewers                     2/3/72
  L:THE MIDNIGHT LADY AND THE MORNING MAN;Converting
    books to film;David Anthony                          2/5/56
  L:Payment plans;Pronzini and Jack Anderson;
    Sander's THE THIRD DEADLY SIN                        4/6/47
  L:Horses;J.Banks;Sex and violence;Nero Wolfe TV
    series;Spelling                                      5/1/45
R:BARETTA(A.Patrick)                                     2/1/40
R:THE BILLION DOLLAR BRAIN(L.Deighton)                   2/1/38
R:THE BLIND SEARCH(L.Egan)                               1/4/47
R:THE BRANDENBURG HOTEL(P.G.Winslow)                     1/2/42
R:BRIGHTLIGHT(T.Bernard)                                 2/1/37
R:BY HOOK OR BY CROOK(E.Lathen)                          1/6/42
R:CIRCLE OF FIRE(M.Sadler)                               1/4/47
R:DEATH AT THE BAR(N.Marsh)                              2/1/40
R:DEATH IN ECSTASY(N.Marsh)                              2/1/37
R:ENTER A MURDERER(N.Marsh)                              2/3/54
R:EVEN THE WICKED(E.McBain)                              1/5/40
R:FAT CHANCE(K.Laumer)                                   2/3/55
R:FELICIA(G.A.Effinger)                                  3/3/46
R:FROM LONDON FAR(M.Innes)                               1/4/48
R:GENTLE ALBATROSS(E.F.Smith)                            1/2/42
R:THE HANGED MEN(D.Harper)                               2/3/54
R:HELL'S FULL(W.Harrison)                                2/6/42
R:HORSE UNDER WATER(L.Deighton)                          2/5/44
R:THE HUNTED(E.Leonard)                                  2/1/35
R:THE JAPANESE CORPSE(J.Van de Wetering)                 2/6/41
R:JUSTICE ENDS AT HOME AND OTHER STORIES(R.Stout)  3/5/43
R:THE KILLERS OF STARFISH(J.Gillis)                      1/6/43
R:THE LAMB WHITE DAYS(F.H.Hall)                          2/1/36
R:THE LAW'S DELAY(S.Woods)                               1/4/48
R:THE MINUTEMAN MURDER(J.Langton)                        1/2/41
R:THE MULTIPLE MAN(B.Bova)                               2/1/35
R:MURDER FOR CHARITY(P.Ponder)                           2/3/55
R:MUSIC TO MURDER BY(V.Hinkle)                           2/5/44
R:THE PATCHWORK MAN(D.Harper)                            2/5/44
R:THE PERFECT CORPSE(L.R.Wright)                         1/4/47
R:THE PLACE OF DEVILS(L.Blair)                           2/1/37
R:THE PRETTY PINK SHROUD(E.X.Ferrars)                    2/6/41
R:THE QUESTION OF MAX(A.Cross)                           2/5/44
```

```
R:THE REINGOLD ROUTE(A.Maling)                          3/5/42
R:THE RENDEZVOUS(E.Anthony)                             2/1/39
R:SCALES OF JUSTICE(N.Marsh)                            2/1/38
R:THE SILVER FALCON(E.Anthony)                          2/6/42
R:A SIMPLE ACT OF KINDNESS(W.M.Estes)                   2/3/56
R:STUD GAME(E.Anthony)                                  2/6/42
R:TEN PLUS ONE(E.McBain)                                1/4/47
R:THE TERMINAL CONNECTION(R.Moore)                      1/5/41
R:THEY FOUND HIM DEAD(G.Heyer)                          1/6/42
R:TUMBLEWEED(J.Van de Wetering)                         1/2/42
R:WHERE THERE'S SMOKE(E.McBain)                         1/5/40
R:THE Z PAPERS(G.I.Simmons)                             1/6/42
Brust,Toby  L:Reading and enjoying TMF;Wolfe & Queen;
    Finding mysteries in bookstores;Joining TMF         4/5/45
Butler,Richard C
    DELL "MAP BACK" CHECKLIST 1-300                     1/2/17
    L:Dell and Popular Library Checklists               1/2/47
    POPULAR LIBRARY PAPERBACK CHECKLIST 1-200           1/3/5
THE CAPER NOVELS OF TONY KENRICK(G.Kelley)              2/4/3
Carr,Wooda Nicholas II JOHN DICKSON CARR(1906-1977)     1/3/3
Carter,Steven R.  FREEDOM AND MYSTERY IN JOHN FOWLES'
    THE ENIGMA                                          3/5/14
Cerasoli,Karl  COVER ART: The Black Bird      FRONT 3/3
CHANCE AND ILLOGIC AND THE BLACK BOX MURDER
    (E.F.Bleiler)                                       2/1/8
A CHINESE DETECTIVE IN SAN FRANCISCO(E.F.Bleiler)       5/3/2
Clark,Jim  L:Mr. and Mrs. North                        1/2/50
Cole,Don
    L:High adventure fiction;Coverage of "today's"
      writers                                           1/5/59
    L:Joe Hensley and his books;New authors and some
      fine new mysteries                                3/1/48
Cook,Michael
    L:Unicorn Mystery Book Club wants                   2/6/60
    L:M.Cook's new book:MURDER BY MAIL:THE HISTORY OF
      MYSTERY BOOK CLUBS WITH COMPLETE CHECKLISTS       3/1/54
    L:Comment on 3/5;Publishing THE NERO WOLFE SAGA;
      Gregarious mystery fans                           4/1/47
    L:MONTHLY MURDERS;Requests for various magazines    5/2/48
    L:MONTHLY MURDERS;FAN FARE                          3/4/46
    R:CRIME,DETECTIVE,ESPIONAGE,MYSTERY,AND THRILLER
      FICTION AND FILM:A COMPREHENSIVE BIBLIOGRAPHY
      OF CRITICAL WRITING THROUGH 1979
      (D. and A. Skene Melvin)                          5/2/30
COVER ART
    Question Mark(G.M.Townsend)                      FRONT/PI
    The Mystery Fancier in Question Marks
      (G.M.Townsend)                                 FRONT 1/1
    Archie and Nero(R.Harris/A.Scott)                FRONT 1/2
    Poe(M.Avallone)                                   BACK 1/2
    Dr.Fell(S.Shiffman)                              FRONT 1/3
    The Dancing Men(G.M.Townsend)                    FRONT 1/4
    The Continuing Character(S.Shiffman)             FRONT 1/5
    The Speckled Band(S.Shiffman)                    FRONT 1/6
    Gun Moll(A.Fick)                      FRONT 2/1,4/4,4/5
    William Powell as Philo Vance                    FRONT 2/2
    Townsend "obit"(G.M.Townsend)                    FRONT 2/3
    Giant Rats of Sumatra(G.M.Townsend)               BACK 2/4
    Ken Crossen(F.Hamilton)                          FRONT 2/5
    The Fallen Body(Mrs.David Doerrer)               FRONT 2/6
```

8

Johnson,Tom   COVER ART: The Mystery Fancier   FRONT 4/6-5/6
THE JOURNAL OF RATIOCINATIVE RESEARCH(J.L.Breen)   1/5/16
Juri,Dorothy
  L:Nero Wolfe movies;Women subscribers   1/5/53
  L:Women's interest in mysteries   2/1/57
Kabatchnik,Amnon
  AGATHA CHRISTIE IS STILL ALIVE AND WELL   2/6/9
  R:'GATOR(G.Ford)   1/3/46
  R:AGATHA CHRISTIE:FIRST LADY OF CRIME(H.R.F.
   Keating)   2/1/32
  R:ALLIGATORS(S.Katz)   1/3/46
  R:THE BLACK CAT(L.Daniels)   2/4/46
  R:THE BLUE HAMMER(R.Macdonald)   1/2/38
  R:BODY RUB(M.Andrews)   1/5/42
  R:CROC'(D.James)   1/3/45
  R:THE CURSE OF THE FLEERS(B.Cooper)   2/1/35
  R:THE DEADLY SPRING(J.C.Conway)   1/5/42
  R:LEW ARCHER,PRIVATE INVESTIGATOR(R.Macdonald)   2/4/47
  R:LOVE KILLS(D.Greenburg)   3/1/42
  R:MAIGRET AND THE HOTEL MAJESTIC(G.Simenon)   2/5/40
  R:THE MOMENT OF TRUTH(K.A.Blom)   1/4/45
  R:ONE FEARFUL YELLOW EYE(J.D.MacDonald)   2/4/48
  R:OPERATION APRICOT(C.A.Haddad)   2/4/46
  R:RAISE THE TITANIC!(C.Cussler)   1/4/44
  R:THE SAVAGE WOMEN(M.Curtis)   1/5/41
  R:SINGLED OUT(S.Whitney)   3/1/42
  R:SNAKE(J.McClure)   1/1/35
  R:THE THETA SYNDROME(E.Trevor)   2/1/34
  R:THE TWENTY-THIRD WEB(R.Himmel)   2/4/45
  R:THE WEREWOLF(B.Cooper)   2/4/47
Kelley,George
  BILL PRONZINI REVISITED   2/5/5
  THE CAPER NOVELS OF TONY KENRICK   2/4/3
  THE CRIME NOVELS OF HAROLD R. DANIELS   3/4/13
  THE DEGENERATION OF DONALD HAMILTON   1/6/11
  THE EXPLOSIVE NOVELS OF RICHARD L. GRAVES   3/6/9
  FEAR AND LOATHING WITH THE LONE WOLF   1/5/17
  L:THE ENCYCLOPEDIA OF MYSTERY AND DETECTION;
   Reviews   1/1/39
  L:Retrospective reviews;Yearly indices   1/4/56
  L:G.Vidal's MATTERS OF FACT AND FICTION:ESSAYS
   1973-1976;Format of books in England   1/5/57
  L:Donald Hamilton's writing;D.Koontz aka B.
   Coffey;Yearly poll   2/2/51
  L:Format and content of TMF over the years   4/1/48
  L:Recommending Roger Sale's ON NOT BEING GOOD
   ENOUGH:WRITINGS OF A WORKING CRITIC   4/2/57
  LOOKING FOR RACHEL WALLACE AND GINGER NORTH   4/3/29
  THE PROGRAMMED WRITING OF DEAN R. KOONTZ   1/4/11
  R:MIDNIGHT SPECIALS:AN ANTHOLOGY FOR TRAIN BUFFS
   AND SUSPENSE AFICIONADOS(B.Pronzini,ed)   1/6/46
  R:BAIT MONEY(M.Collins)   1/6/50
  R:BLOOD MONEY(M.Collins)   1/6/50
  R:THE BROKER(M.Collins)   1/6/50
  R:THE BROKER'S WIFE(M.Collins)   1/6/50
  R:THE DEALER(M.Collins)   1/6/50
  R:THE DEVIL FINDS WORK(M.Delving)   1/6/50
  R:DIE LIKE A MAN(M.Delving)   1/6/50
  R:DIMENSIONS OF DETECTIVE FICTION(L.Landrum/
   P.Browne/R.B.Browne.eds)   1/4/50

```
R:THE CASE OF THE UNCONQUERED SISTERS(T.Downing)    3/4/40
R:CASSIS...RESORT TO VENGEANCE(M.Walker)            3/6/35
R:CAST IN ORDER OF DISAPPEARANCE(S.Brett)           1/1/29
R:CASTLES BURNING(A.Lyons)                          5/1/27
R:THE CAVANAUGH QUEST(T.Gifford)                    1/3/39
R:THE CHAIN OF CHANCE(S.Lem)                        3/5/35
R:THE CHANGELING CONSPIRACY(H.McCloy)               1/6/38
R:CHARITY ENDS AT HOME(C.Watson)                    2/6/34
R:CHARLIE M(B.Freemantle)                           2/3/41
R:CHARLIE'S ANGELS(M.Franklin)                      1/4/39
R:THE CHICAGO GIRL(T.Kenrick)                       1/2/24
R:THE CHIEF INSPECTOR'S DAUGHTER(S.Radley)          5/2/22
R:THE CHINA EXPERT(M.Delving)                       2/1/24
R:THE CHINESE CONSORTIUM(W.Rilla)                   4/5/34
R:A CHOICE OF CRIMES(L.Egan)                        5/2/15
R:CINDERELLA AFTER MIDNIGHT(F.Zackel)               5/1/23
R:THE CINNAMON MURDER(F.Crane)                      1/5/35
R:CITY OF WHISPERING STONE(G.C.Chesbro)             3/1/33
R:A CLASH OF HAWKS(R.Charles)                       PI/23
R:THE CLOCK STRIKES THIRTEEN(H.Brean)               3/4/41
R:CLOSE TO DEATH(J.Crowe)                           3/6/33
R:CLOSET BONES(T.Bunn)                              2/3/46
R:A CLUTCH OF VIPERS(J.S.Scott)                     3/6/38
R:COFFIN COUNTRY(A.M.Stein)                         1/6/39
R:COLD HAND IN MINE(R.Aickman)                      2/6/31
R:COLD TURKEY(T.Childs)                             3/6/30
R:THE COME-ON(M.York)                               3/6/28
R:A CORNER OF PARADISE(L.Holton)                    2/1/22
R:A CORPSE FOR A CANDIDATE(M.Geller)                4/3/39
R:THE CORPSE ON THE DIKE(J.Van de Wetering)         1/1/30
R:THE CORPSE WITH THE DIRTY FACE(R.A.J.Walling)     3/6/33
R:CORRUPT AND ENSNARE(F.M.Nevins,Jr.)               3/1/31
R:COUNTRY AND FATAL(G.Bagby)                        4/4/41
R:THE COWLED MENACE(W.E.Hawkins)                    2/4/35
R:CRAIG AND THE MIDAS TOUCH(K.Benton)               PI/29
R:CRIMES PAST(M.Challis)                            5/2/24
R:THE CRIMSON DEATH(A.J.Small)                      3/2/41
R:CROOKED WOOD(M.Underwood)                         3/3/36
R:THE CROSSWORD MYSTERY(R.B.Gillespie)              5/5/21
R:THE CROWING HEN(R.Davis)                          3/2/40
R:CROWN COURT(J.Follett)                            2/6/32
R:THE CRYSTAL CLEAR GLASS(L.Head)                   2/3/43
R:THE CUMBERLAND DECISION(R.Silverman)              2/3/47
R:THE CURSE OF THE FLEERS(B.Cooper)                 2/3/46
R:THE CYPHER(A.Gordon)                              2/4/32
R:DANGER IN PARADISE(A.S.Fleischman)                5/4/25
R:DARK INTERLUDE(P.Cheyney)                         PI/27
R:THE DEAD ARE DISCREET(A.Lyons)                    PI/29
R:DEAD IN THE MORNING(M.Yorke)                      4/2/20
R:DEAD LOW TIDE(J.D.MacDonald)                      1/3/40
R:DEAD PIGEON ON BEETHOVEN STREET(S.Fuller)         PI/25
R:DEAD RUN(J.FOXX)                                  2/4/34
R:DEAD RUN(R.Lockridge)                             1/1/28
R:DEAD-NETTLE(J.B.Hilton)                           2/5/26
R:THE DEADLY DAMES(M.Douglas)                       1/3/42
R:THE DEADLY MISS ASHLEY(F.C.Davis)                 1/1/28
R:THE DEAL OF THE CENTURY(I.K.Martin)               1/5/33
R:DEATH AFTER BREAKFAST(H.Pentecost)                5/2/19
R:DEATH AND LETTERS(E.Daly)                         5/5/25
R:DEATH AND THE GOOD LIFE(R.Hugo)                   5/3/31
```

```
R:THE DEATH AT YEW CORNER(R.Forrest)                      5/2/24
R:DEATH CAP(J.Thompson)                                   3/1/37
R:DEATH GOES ON SKIS(N.Spain)                             1/6/40
R:DEATH IN ALBERT PARK(L.Bruce)                           4/2/35
R:DEATH IN CONNECTICUT(D.Linzee)                          1/5/33
R:DEATH IN GENTLE GROVE(F.Allan)                           PI/29
R:DEATH IN THE CHANNEL(J.R.L.Anderson)                    3/2/36
R:DEATH IS A FRIEND(D.MacKenzie)                          1/5/34
R:DEATH MEETS 400 RABBITS(A.M.Stein)                      5/1/27
R:DEATH NOTES(R.Rendell)                                  5/6/38
R:DEATH OF A DELEGATE(G.Cronin)                           3/6/38
R:DEATH OF A LOW-HANDICAP MAN(B.Ball)                     3/2/36
R:DEATH OF A PERFECT MOTHER(R.Barnard)                    5/6/38
R:DEATH OF A THIN-SKINNED ANIMAL(P.Alexander)             2/4/36
R:DEATH OF AN EXPERT WITNESS(P.D.James)                   2/3/47
R:DEATH ON LOCATION(W.R.Cox)                              3/2/38
R:DEATH STALK(B.Langley)                                  3/6/27
R:DEATH UNDER PAR(J.Law)                                  5/3/32
R:DEATH'S SWEET SONG(C.Adams)                             2/2/35
R:DEATH,MY DARLING DAUGHTER(J.Stagge)                     2/4/32
R:DECEIT AND DEADLY LIES(F.Bandy)                         3/3/33
R:DECOYS(R.Hoyt)                                          5/2/14
R:A DEMON IN MY VIEW(R.Rendell)                           1/3/37
R:THE DESTROYER
        #26:IN ENEMY HANDS(R.Sapir/W.Murphy)              1/2/28
        #31:THE HEAD-MEN(R.Sapir/W.Murphy)                2/4/33
        #37:THE BOTTOM LINE(R.Sapir/W.Murphy)             3/6/31
R:DEVINE DEATH(L.Derrick)                                 2/1/26
R:DIAMOND STUD(N.Singer)                                  1/2/28
R:DIAMONDS IN THE DUMPLINGS(S.Shane)                      3/4/39
R:DIE AFTER DARK(H.Pentecost)                             1/3/38
R:DIE LITTLE GOOSE(D.Alexander)                           2/1/30
R:THE DIEHARD(J.A.Jackson)                                2/1/25
R:DIRTY LAUNDRY(P.Hamil)                                  3/5/37
R:DIRTY TRICKS(P.Way)                                     2/4/31
R:DOCTOR,LAWYER...(C.Wilcox)                              2/1/23
R:THE DOOR TO DOOM AND OTHER DETECTIONS(J.D.Carr)         4/5/35
R:DOUBLE OR QUITS(A.A.Fair)                               1/2/23
R:DR.JEKYLL AND MR.HOLMES(J.Watson/L.D.Estleman,
    ed)                                                   4/2/34
R:DRAGON HUNT(D.J.Garrity)                                4/2/38
R:DULCIE BLIGH(G.Clark)                                   2/5/27
R:THE DUVEEN LETTER(E.Leather)                            4/5/33
R:EARLY AUTUMN(R.B.Parker)                                5/2/25
R:EDWIN OF THE IRON SHOES(M.Muller)                       2/3/48
R:EIGHTY DOLLARS TO STAMFORD(L.Fletcher)                   PI/25
R:THE EMERALD(M.Carrel)                                   4/4/36
R:THE EMPTY COPPER SEA(J.D.MacDonald)                     3/6/38
R:THE EMPTY HOUSE(M.Gilbert)                              3/6/31
R:ENDPLAY(R.G.Toepfer)                                    2/1/29
R:THE ENIGMA(M.Barak)                                     3/1/36
R:THE ENTHUSIAST(P.Hill)                                  3/6/28
R:EVERY INCH A LADY(J.Fleming)                            2/6/32
R:EVIDENCE(J.Wiseman)                                     5/6/39
R:THE EVIL GNOME(K.Robeson)                                PI/24
R:AN EXCELLENT NIGHT FOR MURDER(V.Rath)                   3/6/36
R:EXIT SHERLOCK HOLMES(R.L.Hall)                          1/5/31
R:THE EYES OF BUDDHA(J.Ball)                              1/3/40
R:FAGO(B.Roueche)                                         2/3/43
R:THE FARNSWORTH SCORE(R.Burns)          -                1/5/29
```

R:THE FASCINATOR(A.York)   1/5/35
R:FELECIA(G.A.Effinger)   1/2/24
R:FESTIVAL(J.Anderson)   4/2/37
R:THE FIELDS OF EDEN(M.T.Hinkemeyer)   3/1/33
R:FIND A CROOKED SIXPENCE(E.Thompson)   2/5/26
R:FIND SHERRI!(P.Swan)   4/3/36
R:FINGERS OF DEATH(M.Grant)   2/1/26
R:FIVE ROADS TO DEATH(J.Philips)   2/5/31
R:THE FLESH WAS COLD(B.Fischer)   1/1/27
R:FLETCH(G.Mcdonald)   1/3/37
R:THE FLEUR-DE-LIS AFFAIR(H.Ross)   1/1/30
R:THE FLOWERED BOX(T.J.Green)   5/2/20
R:FOREVER WILT THOU DIE(B.N.Byfield)   2/5/32
R:FREE FALL IN CRIMSON(J.D.MacDonald)   5/4/23
R:FREEBOOTY(J.Foxx)   1/2/23
R:A FRIEND IN DEED(R.Jagoda)   2/4/33
R:FROG IN THE THROAT(E.X.Ferrars)   5/2/23
R:THE GAMBLER.THE MINSTREL,AND THE DANCE HALL
   QUEEN(W.Downing)   1/1/30
R:GAMESKEEPER'S GALLOWS(J.B.Hilton)   1/6/38
R:GAMES(B.Pronzini)   1/2/25
R:GENINI TRIP(J.Law)   2/1/26
R:GIDEON'S DRIVE(J.J.Marric)   2/1/28
R:THE GIRL BETWEEN(B.Fischer)   3/2/38
R:THE GLASS TRIANGLE(G.H.Coxe)   1/5/36
R:THE GLENDOWER LEGACY(T.Gifford)   3/3/34
R:THE GLIMPSES OF THE MOON(E.Crispin)   5/1/20
R:THE GLORY GAME(S.Williamson)   2/4/30
R:GO WEST,INSPECTOR GHOTE(H.R.F.Keating)   5/6/33
R:GOD SAVE THE CHILD(R.B.Parker)   3/4/39
R:GOING FOR THE GOLD(E.Lathen)   5/3/32
R:THE GOLD OF TROY(R.L.Fish)   5/1/25
R:THE GONE MAN(B.Solomon)   2/2/35
R:GONE NO FORWARDING(J.Gores)   2/5/28
R:GOOD LUCK MISTER(B.Freeborn)   1/4/37
R:GOOD NIGHT AND GOOD-BYE(T.Harris)   5/3/31
R:GOODBYE GEORGEOUS(K.Campbell)   5/2/18
R:THE GOSPEL LAMB(J.S.Scott)   5/3/29
R:THE GOLDEN FLEECE(R.Obstfeld)   3/6/34
R:THE GRAIL TREE(J.Gash)   4/5/34
R:THE GRAND MODENA MURDER(L.R.Gribble)   3/4/39
R:GRAVE ERROR(S.Greenleaf)   5/4/23
R:GREEN EYES(M.Grant)   1/3/42
R:GUARANTEED TO FADE(G.Bagby)   3/4/38
R:HALO FOR SATAN(J.Evans)   4/3/41
R:THE HANDS OF HEALING MURDER(B.D'Amato)   5/2/21
R:THE HANGED MEN(D.Harper)   1/2/28
R:THE HARD BOILED DETECTIVE:STORIES FROM BLACK
   MASK MAGAZINE   1/2/35
R:HARD TO KILL(J.Marcott)   PI/26
R:HARD TRADE(A.Lyons)   5/4/24
R:HATCHETT(L.McGraw)   1/2/26
R:HEADLESS VICTORY(D.D.Lifson)   3/3/38
R:HERE COMES CHARLIE M.(B.Freemantle)   3/4/38
R:HIGH PLACES(P.Ferris)   1/5/30
R:HIGH WIDE AND RANSOME(D.Tracy)   1/2/28
R:HONEYBATH'S HAVEN(M.Innes)   2/5/29
R:HOODWINK(B.Pronzini)   5/5/27
R:HOOKERS DON'T GO TO HEAVEN(L.V.Roper)   1/2/26
R:HOSTAGE TO DEATH(J.Ashford)   2/5/26

```
R:THE HOUR OF THE OXRUN DEAD(C.L.Grant)              2/3/41
R:HOUSE OF FLESH(B.Fischer)                          3/6/32
R:THE HOWARD HUGHES AFFAIR(S.Kaminsky)               3/6/40
R:THE HUMAN ZERO:THE SCIENCE FICTION STORIES OF
   ERLE STANLEY GARDNER(E.S.Gardner)                 5/2/13
R:HUNTER OF THE BLOOD(W.Masterson)                   1/5/30
R:HUNTERS IN THE DARK(E.Thompson)                    3/6/28
R:THE HUNTERS(P.Hill)                                1/3/37
R:I COULD HAVE DIED(G.Bagby)                         3/5/39
R:I HAVE GLORIA KIRBY(R.Himmel)                      2/5/34
R:THE IBIZIA SYNDICATE(B.Reade)                      2/1/29
R:IF I DON'T TELL(D.Olson)                           PI/27
R:IF YOU WANT A MURDER WELL DONE(M.Scherf)           PI/26
R:THE IMPOSTER(H.McCloy)                             2/1/24
R:IN THE LAMB WHITE DAYS(F.H.Hall)                   PI/30
R:AN INCIDENT IN ICELAND(N.Webster)                  4/2/32
R:INCLINATION TO MURDER(H.Hunter)                    3/6/33
R:THE INVISIBLE FLAMINI(C.Brown)                     3/5/38
R:THE JANUS MURDER(J.N.Datesh)                       3/5/40
R:THE JAPANESE CORPSE(J.Van de Wetering)             2/5/28
R:JOURNEY TO A SAFE PLACE(I.S.Black)                 4/2/39
R:THE JUDAS GOAT(R.B.Parker)                         3/3/37
R:THE JUDAS PAIR(J.Gash)                             2/3/47
R:THE KAMA SUTRA TANGO(J.F.Burke)                    2/1/22
R:KEY WEST CONNECTION(R.Striker)                     5/3/27
R:A KILLING FOR CHARITY(A.Kaplan)                    PI/27
R:A KILLING IN SWORDS(R.Bretnor)                     2/6/31
R:THE KILLING KIND(E.West)                           2/4/33
R:THE KILLING OF KATIE STEELSTOCK(M.Gilbert)         4/5/30
R:KISS YOUR ELBOW(A.Handley)                         3/6/37
R:KISSES LEAVE NO FINGERPRINTS(M.Fredman)            4/5/32
R:THE KNIFE WILL FALL(M.Cumberland)                  5/2/16
R:KNOCKDOWN(D.Francis)                               1/3/40
R:LABYRINTH(B.Pronzini)                              4/3/38
R:THE LADY IN BLACK(A.Clarke)                        2/5/30
R:THE LADY LOVED TOO WELL(J.Donahue)                 2/5/28
R:THE LADY OF DARKNESS(R.Rendell)                    5/1/22
R:THE LASKO TANGENT(R.N.Patterson)                   4/5/31
R:THE LAST GOOD KISS(J.Crumley)                      3/3/31
R:THE LAW'S DELAY(S.Woods)                           1/5/29
R:THE LEGEND(E.Anthony)                              1/1/32
R:LETTERS FROM THE PAST(A.Clarke)                    5/5/21
R:LIES(R.Neely)                                      2/5/29
R:THE LIME PIT(J.Valin)                              4/4/35
R:LIVE BAIT(B.Knox)                                  3/6/30
R:LIVING IMAGE(G.S.Gallant)                          3/1/35
R:A LONELY WAY TO DIE(A.Bourgeau)                    4/5/29
R:LOOK BACK ON DEATH(L.Egan)                         3/3/36
R:LOOKING FOR RACHEL WALLACE(R.B.Parker)             4/3/34
R:THE LOOKING GLASS MURDER(P.Lore)                   4/5/29
R:LOVE KILLS(D.Greenburg)                            3/1/31
R:THE LUNATIC FRINGE(W.L.DeAndrea)                   5/1/24
R:THE LUXEMBOURG RUN(S.Ellin)                        2/3/44
R:THE MACKIN COVER(D.K.Shah)                         2/2/34
R:MAJOR ENQUIRY(L.Henderson)                         1/1/27
R:THE MAKASSAR STRAIT CONTRACT(P.Altee)              1/3/40
R:MAKING HATE(J.Wilson)                              2/6/33
R:THE MALTESE FALCON(D.Hammett)                      5/3/31
R:THE MAN ON THE BRIDGE(T.S.Black)                   2/1/27
R:THE MAN WHO DIED TWICE(S.A.Peeples)                1/3/41
```

```
R:THE MAN WHO KILLED HIS BROTHER(R.Stephens)        5/2/17
R:THE MAN WITH BOGART'S FACE(A.J.Fenady)            1/3/39
R:THE MAN WITH FIFTY COMPLAINTS(M.McMullen)         3/5/36
R:THE MAN WITH THE TATOOED FACE(M.Burton)           4/4/41
R:THE MARAUDERS(G.R.Shirreffs)                      1/3/41
R:MCGARR AND THE SCIENCE CONSPIRACY(B.Gill)         3/1/32
R:MCGARR ON THE CLIFFS OF MOHER(B.Gill)             3/3/39
R:MCQUAID IN AUGUST(S.Rifkin)                       3/6/29
R:MEANS OF EVIL(R.Rendell)                          4/3/34
R:THE MEMORIAL HALL MURDER(J.Langton)               3/1/34
R:THE MEN ON THE DEAD MAN'S CHEST(C.Raymond)        2/5/32
R:THE MEXICAN ASSASSIN(Hartshorne)                  2/6/30
R:MICHAEL SHAYNE'S LONG CHANCE(B.Halliday)          2/4/32
R:MIKE DIME(B.Fantoni)                              5/4/26
R:MIND OVER MURDER(W.X.Kienzle)                     5/4/22
R:MINISTRY OF DEATH(J.Bingham)                      2/5/26
R:MINOR MURDERS(J.L.Hensley)                        4/2/36
R:MISSING WOMAN(M.Z.Lewin)                          5/6/39
R:MIZMAZE(M.Fitt)                                   5/3/28
R:THE MOMENT OF FICTION(D.Estow)                    3/6/30
R:MONA(L.Block)                                     3/2/38
R:MOONLIGHT AT GREYSTONE(L.Bronte)                  1/1/31
R:A MORBID TASTE FOR BONES(E.Peters)                4/4/37
R:THE MORGUE THE MERRIER(J.Truesdale)               3/6/39
R:THE MORIDA MAN(R.Thomas)                          5/6/34
R:THE MOROCCAN(C.A.Haddad)                          3/3/33
R:MOTIVE IN SHADOW(L.Egan)                          4/2/40
R:MOTOR CITY BLUES(L.D.Estleman)                    5/3/27
R:MOUCHE(Demouzon)                                  5/2/21
R:MUGGER'S DAY(G.Bagby)                             3/6/39
R:A MURDER ARRANGED(J.Philips)                      3/3/37
R:MURDER AT ELAINE'S(R.Rosenbaum)                   3/5/39
R:MURDER AT HIGH TIDE(C.G.Booth)                    3/4/40
R:MURDER AT THE RED OCTOBER(A.Olcott)               5/6/41
R:MURDER AT THE UN(W.Perry)                         1/1/33
R:MURDER AT THE VILLA ROSA(A.E.W.Mason)             4/5/28
R:MURDER BEGETS MURDER(R.Jefferies)                 4/2/32
R:MURDER FOR CHARITY(P.Ponder)                      2/4/31
R:MURDER IS A GAMBLE(G.M.Barnes)                    1/1/28
R:THE MURDER MAKERS(J.Rossiter)                     1/6/39
R:MURDER MYSTERY(G.Thompson)                        5/2/18
R:MURDER OF A MYSTERY WRITER(E.Heath)               3/2/39
R:A MURDER OF CROWS(P.Buchanan)                     1/1/28
R:THE MURDER OF MIRANDA(M.Millar)                   3/6/29
R:THE MURDER OF THE MAHARAJAH(H.R.F.Keating)        4/4/40
R:MURDER ON DISPLAY(C.Hale)                         4/3/40
R:MURDER ON MARTHA'S VINEYARD(K.Roos)               5/5/23
R:MURDER ON THE YELLOW BRICK ROAD(S.Kaminsky)       2/6/32
R:MURDER R.F.D.(L.Stephan)                          2/5/27
R:MURDER SO REAL(A.Bird)                            3/1/35
R:MURDER WITH LOVE(V.Howard)                        5/6/36
R:MURDER WITHOUT WEAPONS(A.B.Cunningham)            3/2/40
R:MURDER.MURDER LITTLE STAR(M.Babson)               4/3/34
R:MURDERER'S ROW(A.Hitchcock,ed)                    1/1/33
R:MY FOE OUTSTRETCH'D BENEATH THE TREE
    (V.C.Clinton-Baddeley)                          3/1/37
R:MY GUN IS QUICK(M.Spillane)                       PI/28
R:MY LIFE IS DONE(S.Woods)                          1/4/38
R:MYSTERY OF THE ANGRY IDOL(P.A.Whitney)            2/6/34
R:MYSTERY VILLA(E.R.Punshon)                        5/6/34
```

```
R:THE NECKLACE OF SKULLS(I.Drummond)              1/6/39
R:THE NEON GRAVEYARD(G.Baxt)                      4/2/31
R:THE NEON PREACHER(R.Chambers)                   2/3/45
R:NEVER CROSS A VAMPIRE(S.Kaminsky)               5/1/21
R:NEVER SAY DIE(E.Foote-Smith)                    2/1/24
R:THE NICE MURDERS(D.Delman)                      2/1/22
R:NIGHT COVER(M.Z.Lewin)                          4/4/39
R:NIGHT OF THE JABBERWOCK(F.Brown)                3/6/40
R:THE NIGHT PEOPLE(J.Finney)                      2/3/41
R:THE NIGHT SHE DIED(D.Simpson)                   5/5/22
R:THE NIGHT RUNNERS(M.Collins)                    2/6/33
R:NO BUSINESS BEING A COP(L.O'Donnell)            3/5/36
R:NO CERTAIN LIFE(R.Neely)                        2/5/31
R:NO SECOND WIND(A.B.Guthrie,Jr.)                 4/3/36
R:NOBODY'S PERFECT(D.E.Westlake)                  5/1/22
R:NOT SLEEPING,JUST DEAD(C.Alverson)              2/2/34
R:NOTHING BUT FOXES(R.Lewis)                      3/5/38
R:THE OCTOBER CABERET(E.Quest)                    3/6/41
R:OGILVIE,TALLANT AND MOON(C.Q.Yarbro)            1/4/39
R:OH,BURY ME NOT(M.K.Wren)                        2/5/32
R:THE OLD DICK(L.A.Morse)                         5/6/40
R:THE OLD DIE YOUNG(R.Lockridge)                  5/1/25
R:ONCE UPON A CRIME(C.Monig)                      PI/23
R:ONE CORPSE TOO MANY(E.Peters)                   4/4/34
R:ONE DEAD DEBUTANTE(H.Gould)                     1/2/23
R:ONE DIP DEAD(A.M.Stein)                         3/6/35
R:ONE TEAR FOR MY GRAVE(M.Roscoe)                 2/5/33
R:ONE WREATH WITH LOVE(J.Roffman)                 3/3/31
R:THE OPEN SHADOW(B.Solomon)                      3/6/27
R:OPIUM FLOWER(D.Cushman)                         PI/25
R:THE ORIGINAL CARCASE(G.Bagby)                   2/4/34
R:OUTSIDE IN(M.Z.Lewin)                           4/5/33
R:OVER THE EDGE(S.Kemp)                           3/6/37
R:A PACKET FULL OF TROUBLE(F.U.Ashford)           5/4/25
R:THE PALACE GUARD(C.MacLeod)                     5/5/26
R:THE PAPERBACK PRICE GUIDE(K.Hancer)             5/1/28
R:PAPERBAG(R.Russell)                             4/2/32
R:A PARCEL OF THEIR FORTUNES(B.N.Byfield)         4/2/38
R:THE PASSENGER FROM SCOTLAND YARD(H.F.Wood)      2/5/30
R:PASSING STRANGE(C.Aird)                         5/4/21
R:PASSPORT TO PERIL(R.Parker)                     1/4/40
R:PAY ON THE WAY OUT(J.Murphy)                    1/1/27
R:PEKING DUCK(R.Simon)                            3/6/32
R:THE PEKING MAN IS MISSING(C.Taschidigan)        2/2/33
R:THE PENNY MURDERS(L.Black)                      5/1/23
R:PHOENIX NO MORE(E.Gage)                         3/1/36
R:PHOTO FINISH(N.Marsh)                           5/1/26
R:PICTURE MISS SEETON(H.Carvic)                   1/4/38
R:A PINT OF MURDER(A.Craig)                       4/4/42
R:PLOT IT YOURSELF(R.Stout)                       PI/23
R:POOL OF TEARS(J.Wainright)                      2/3/43
R:PORT ARTHUR CHICKEN(T.Chiu)                     4/2/36
R:POUR THE HEMLOCK(A.J.Russell)                   1/3/37
R:POWER PLAYS(C.Wilcox)                           3/6/29
R:PROMISED LAND(R.B.Parker)                       1/1/32
R:PUBLIC MURDERS(B.Granger)                       4/3/35
R:PURE SWEET HELL(M.Douglas)                      PI/29
R:PUZZLE FOR FIENDS(P.Quentin)                    4/4/40
R:THE QUIET RIVER(P.M.Hubbard)                    3/3/37
R:QUOTH THE RAVEN(B.Fischer)                      1/2/25
```

```
R:RALLY TO KILL(B.Knox)                                      1/5/36
R:THE RANDOM FACTOR(L.J.LaRosa/B.Tanenbaum)                  3/1/33
R:RANDOM KILLER(H.Pentecost)                                 3/6/29
R:RAVEN AND THE KAMIKAZE(D.MacKenzie)                        2/4/36
R:RECOIL(B.Garfield)                                         1/5/34
R:THE RED CASTLE MYSTERY(H.C.Bailey)                         1/5/35
R:RED IS FOR SHROUDS(M.A.Taylor)                             5/4/21
R:THE RED-LIGHT VICTIM(L.Kinsley)                            5/5/24
R:REMAINS TO BE SEEN(M.Butterworth)                          2/4/35
R:REPRISAL(W.P.McGivern)                                     4/2/34
R:REST YOU MERRY(C.MacLeod)                                  3/5/36
R:THE RETALIATORS(D.Hamilton)                                1/1/30
R:REVEREND RANDOLLPH AND THE AVENGING ANGEL
   (C.M.Smith)                                               2/6/30
R:REVEREND RANDOLLPH AND THE FALL FROM GRACE,INC.
   (C.M.Smith)                                               3/4/38
R:THE RICH GET IT ALL(F.Huston)                              3/6/33
R:A RICH WAY TO DIE(K.Evans)                                 3/6/40
R:ROAST EGGS(D.Clark)                                        5/6/36
R:THE ROLLING HEADS(A.M.Stein)                               3/6/28
R:THE ROSARY MURDERS(W.X.Kienzle)                            3/5/40
R:ROUSE THE DEVIL(C.Weston)                                  1/1/29
R:RUBOUT AT THE ONYX(H.P.Jeffers)                            5/6/37
R:RULLING PASSION(R.Hill)                                    2/3/42
R:A RUN IN DIAMONDS(A.Saxon)                                 1/6/40
R:SABINE(N.Freeling)                                         3/2/36
R:THE SAINT AND THE TEMPLAR TREASURE(L.Charteris)            3/6/31
R:SAND DOLLARS(R.Terrall)                                    3/3/34
R:A SAVAGE PLACE(R.B.Parker)                                 5/5/25
R:SAY IT AIN'T SO.GORDON LITTLEFIELD(E.Asinof)               2/3/45
R:SCARED TO DEATH(A.Morice)                                  2/4/32
R:SCARLET NIGHT(D.S.Davis)                                   4/4/39
R:SCHROEDER'S GAME(A.Maling)                                 1/5/29
R:SCRATCHPROOF(M.Maguire)                                    1/6/38
R:THE SCREWBALL KING MURDER(K.Platt)                         2/6/33
R:THE SEASON OF THE MACHETE(J.Patterson)                     2/4/31
R:SECRETS OF THE WORLD'S BEST-SELLING WRITER
   (F.L.Fugate/R.B.Fugate)                                   5/2/13
R:SECRETS(F.L.Bailey)                                        3/3/33
R:SERGEANT RITCHIE'S CONSCIENCE(F.Branston)                  3/5/35
R:THE SERN CHARTER(F.Wyck)                                    PI/30
R:SERVICE OF ALL THE DEAD(C.Dexter)                          4/3/35
R:THE SEVEN DEADLY SISTERS(P.McGerr)                         3/5/38
R:SHAKEDOWN FOR MURDER(E.Lacy)                               PI/27
R:THE SHAKEDOWN KID(N.Singer)                                1/2/27
R:THE SHALLOW GRAVE(J.S.Scott)                               3/1/34
R:SHANGHAI FLAME(A.S.Fleischman)                             2/4/30
R:SHE'LL HATE ME TOMORROW(R.Deming)                          PI/28
R:SHERBOURNE'S FOLLY(N.Barry)                                3/3/39
R:SHROUD FOR A NIGHTINGALE(P.D.James)                        PI/24
R:THE SILENT WORLD OF NICHOLAS QUINN(C.Dexter)               2/2/34
R:THE SILVER CASTLE(E.Quest)                                 3/3/36
R:SINGLED OUT(S.Whitney)                                     3/3/32
R:THE SINS OF THE FATHERS(L.Block)                           2/4/30
R:SLAY THE MURDERER(H.Holman)                                PI/24
R:SLEEP BEFORE EVENING(D.Olson)                              4/2/35
R:A SLEEPING LIFE(R.Rendell)                                 3/3/38
R:THE SLEEPING SPHINX(J.D.Carr)                              2/5/34
R:SLOW DOWN THE WORLD(J.Ashford)                             2/1/28
R:SLOWLY THE LAW(J.Drummond)                                 2/1/29
```

```
R:SMEAR JOB(J.Mitchell)                                    2/3/44
R:SNIPE HUNT(A.Dean)                                       3/4/40
R:SOME RUN CROOKED(J.B.Hilton)                             3/1/34
R:THE SOUND OF MIDNIGHT(C.L.Grant)                         3/3/37
R:SPEAK FOR THE DEAD(R.Burns)                              3/1/34
R:SPENCE AND THE HOLIDAY MURDERS(M.Allen)                  3/3/34
R:SPENCE AT THE BLUE BAZAAR(M.Allen)                       3/6/37
R:THE SPIDER ORCHID(C.Fremlin)                             2/6/30
R:SPLIT ON RED(W.Hughes)                                   5/6/33
R:SPY AND DIE(M.Meyers)                                    1/2/24
R:STAR LIGHT,STAR BRIGHT(S.Ellin)                          4/3/38
R:STAR TRAP(S.Brett)                                       2/5/27
R:THE STEEL PALACE(H.Pentecost)                            3/1/32
R:STEP IN THE DARK(E.Lemarchand)                           2/1/23
R:THE STIFF UPPER LIP(P.Israel)                            3/4/38
R:STING OF THE HONEYBEE(F.Parrish)                       ..4/2/31
R:STRAIGHT(S.Knickmeyer)                                   1/2/27
R:A STRANGE PLACE FOR MURDER(C.Barroll)                    3/6/34
R:THE STRAWBERRY-BLOND JUNGLE(C.Brown)                     3/6/35
R:THE STRIPPER(C.Brown)                                    1/5/34
R:STUD GAME(D.Anthony)                                     3/3/35
R:SUDDENLY WHILE GARDENING(E.Lemarchand)                   3/6/27
R:SUICIDE SEAT(N.Carter)                                   4/5/32
R:SUNK WITHOUT A TRACE(D.Devine)                           4/2/31
R:SUSPICIONS(B.Betcherman)                                 4/4/38
R:SWEET REVENGE(T.Racina)                                  2/4/30
R:SWING,SWING TOGETHER(P.Lovesey)                          1/1/27
R:THE SWITCH(E.Leonard)                                    3/3/35
R:TAKE A STEP TO MURDER(D.Keene)                           PI/26
R:THE TANGENT FACTOR(L.Sanders)                            2/5/30
R:THE TASTE OF FEAR(H.Lamp,ed)                             2/1/28
R:THE TAURUS TRIP(T.B.Dewey)                               PI/24
R:TEN DAYS,MISTER CAIN?(B.Freeborn)                        2/6/32
R:A TERRIBLE TIME TO DIE(T.Scaduto)                        3/1/35
R:THE TERROR SYNDICATE(D.Seaman)                           1/4/38
R:TEXAS WIND(J.M.Reasoner)                                 5/5/26
R:THEN CAME VIOLENCE(J.Ball)                               4/3/39
R:THIS GUN FOR GLORIA(B.Mara)                              PI/23
R:THE THOMAS BERRYMAN NUMBER(J.Patterson)                  1/5/33
R:THREE COUSINS DIE(J.Rhode)                               3/2/39
R:THREE MOTIVES FOR MURDER(R.Winsor)                       1/2/26
R:TIGER BY THE TAIL(L.Goldman)                             3/5/37
R:TO DIE ELSEWHERE(T.Wilden)                               2/1/29
R:TO KEEP OR KILL(W.Tucker)                                5/3/28
R:TO MAKE AN UNDERWORLD(J.Fleming)                         1/1/33
R:THE TOFF AMONG THE MILLIONS(J.Creasey)                   3/2/36
R:TOP STORY MURDER(A.Berkeley)                             1/1/32
R:THE TOUGH GET GOING(G.Bagby)                             2/6/33
R:TOUGH LUCK L.A.(M.Sinclair)                              5/2/17
R:THE TRANS-ATLANTIC GHOST(D.Gardner)                      3/5/41
R:TREASURE BY DEGREES(D.Williams)                          2/5/26
R:TRIAL RUN(D.Francis)                                     3/6/30
R:TROUBLE AT TURKEY HILL(K.M.Knight)                       3/4/41
R:TURKISH WHITE(M.Arrighi)                                 2/1/23
R:TWENTIETH CENTURY CRIME AND MYSTERY WRITERS
   (J.M.Reilly,ed)                                         4/5/27
R:TWO IN THE BUSH(G.Bagby)                                 PI/25
R:TWOSPOT(B.Pronzini/C.Wilcox)                             3/1/36
R:TYGER AT BAY(A.Riefe)                                    PI/26
R:TYGER BY THE TAIL(A.Riefe)                               PI/29
```

AN INDEX OF BOOKS REVIEWED IN TMF VOLUME I
(INCLUCING THE PREVIEW ISSUE)   2/1/9
L:Preview Issue   1/1/45
L:A.M.Stein;Newgate Callendar   1/2/48
L:Ken Crossen checklist;Multiple reviews   1/3/56
L:Comments on article and letters;Avon classic
  crime collection   1/4/58
L:Trevanian;Wooster;Nevins   1/5/55
L:Collectors and readers;Nevins' Gardner/
  Mason reviews   1/6/57
L:Collecting;Comments on reviews,articles,letters 2/2/46
L:Number of letters in TMF;Hon Con;Writing for
  mystery journals;London's bookstores   2/3/69
L:Suggestions for articles;Book buying in England;
  Newgate Callendar;P.D.James on TV   2/4/54
L:Advice for buying books in England;Titles in
  the Hodder/Fawcett Coronet series   2/5/54
L:Banks;Mertz;C.J.Daly;The Hutchinson Crime Book
  Society series;Sturgeon   2/6/48
L:Wooster on Queen authorship;Tim Corrigan;
  Suggestions for articles   3/1/57
L:DEATH ON THE NILE film;THE RED RIGHT HAND   3/2/53
L:T.Sturgeon   3/4/60
R:THE AFFAIR OF THE BLOOD-STAINED EGG COSY
  (J.Anderson)   1/5/42
R:THE AMBUSHERS(D.Hamilton)   1/2/38
R:THE CAVANAUGH QUEST(T.Gifford)   1/3/44
R:CIRCLE OF FIRE(M.Sadler)   1/3/47
R:CONFESS FLETCH(G.Mcdonald)   1/5/37
R:THE CROOKED HINGE(J.D.Carr)   1/4/41
R:CUTTER AND BONE(N.Thornburg)   1/4/43
R:DEATH OF A NURSE(E.McBain)   1/4/44
R:THE DESTROYER(R.Sapir/W.Murphy)
  #4:MAFIA FIX   1/6/52
  #17:LAST WAR DANCE   1/3/48
  #19:HOLY TERROR   1/3/49
R:EVEN THE WICKED(E.McBain)   1/4/44
R:FLETCH(G.Mcdonald)   1/5/37
R:THE FRENCH KEY MYSTERY(F.Gruber)   1/5/47
R:GUILTY BYSTANDER(W.Miller)   1/5/49
R:THE HARD BOILED DETECTIVE:AN ANTHOLOGY AND
  STUDY OF PULP DETECTIVE FICTION(R.Goulart,ed)   1/2/37
R:HEIST ME HIGHER(B.S.Ballinger)   1/4/52
R:IN THE MIDST OF DEATH(L.Block)   1/2/22
R:MURDERER'S ROW(D.Hamilton)   1/5/50
R:THE NAKED FACE(S.Sheldon)   1/3/47
R:NIGHTMARE IN PINK(J.D.MacDonald)   1/3/48
R:AN OXFORD TRAGEDY(J.C.Masterman)   2/2/38
R:THE RAVAGERS(D.Hamilton)   1/2/38
R:RAYMOND CHANDLER SPEAKING(R.Chandler)   1/6/45
R:THE REMOVERS(D.Hamilton)   1/4/53
R:RIM OF THE PIT(H.Talbot)   1/5/49
R:THE SAINT IN NEW YORK(L.Charteris)   1/5/46
R:SAM 7(R.Cox)   2/3/50
R:THE SINS OF THE FATHERS(L.Block)   1/2/22
R:THE SOUR LEMON SCORE(R.Stark)   1/6/51
R:STORM WARNING(J.Higgins)   1/2/40
R:STRAIGHT(S.Knickmeyer)   1/2/16
R:A STUDY IN TERROR(E.Queen)   2/3/56
R:A THREE PIPE PROBLEM(J.Symons)   1/3/48

THE GREAT LIZZIE BORDEN T-SHIRT MEDIA EVENT AND
  MYSTERY QUIZ   5/6/7
L:Copyright laws and quoting;A.M.Stein   1/2/47
L:Western detective stories   1/3/55
L:J.D.Carr;Differing reactions to books   1/4/57
L:Wooster;TRAGEDY OF X checklist;ROYAL BLOODLINE 2/5/50
L:L.French;"Red Mask Mysteries";Wolfe film   3/1/55
L:Simultaneous death law   3/2/59
L:Disney's Jeff Dimarco on old TV   3/4/56
L:Ideal casting choices for Wolfe and Archie   3/5/46
L:Lachman's reviews of Nevins;Seminar on law in
  popular fiction and film   4/2/59
L:Little old men;Melville Fairr   4/5/45
L:TMF prices;Philo Vance   4/6/47
L:Wolfe TV series;Conrad,Horsley and Miller   5/1/44
L:Missing the Wolfe TV show;Robert L. Fish   5/2/50
L:G.Thompson's MURDER MYSTERY;Radio play "A
  Razor in Fleet Street"   5/3/46
L:Lachman's article on Stout and the presidency 5/4/43
R:ACTS OF MERCY(B.Pronzini/B.N.Malzberg)   2/5/37
R:AS HER WHIMSEY TOOK HER:CRITICAL ESSAYS ON
  DOROTHY L.SAYERS(M.P.Hannay,ed)   3/5/45
R:THE BEDSIDE,BATHTUB & ARMCHAIR COMPANION TO
  AGATHA CHRISTIE(D.Riley/P.McAllister,eds) 4/1/33
R:BLOODHOUNDS OF HEAVEN:THE DETECTIVE IN ENGLISH
  FICTION FROM GODWIN TO DOYLE(I.Ousby)   1/4/49
R:BOGMAIL(P.McGinley)   5/5/29
R:THE BUGLES BLOWING(N.Freeling)   1/5/44
R:BUYER BEWARE(J.Lutz)   1/3/43
R:THE CASE OF THE
    AMOROUS AUNT(E.S.Gardner)   1/3/49
    BEAUTIFUL·BEGGAR(E.S.Gardner)   1/4/54
    BIGAMOUS SPOUSE(E.S.Gardner)   1/1/37
    BLOOD BONANZA(E.S.Gardner)   1/2/10
    CARELESS CUPID(E.S.Gardner)   1/5/50
    DARING DIVORCEE(E.S.Gardner)   1/3/49
    FABULOUS FAKE(E.S.Gardner)   1/5/51
    HORRIFIED HEIRS(E.S.Gardner)   1/3/50
    ICE COLD HANDS(E.S.Gardner)   1/2/45
    MISCHIEVOUS DOLL(E.S.Gardner)   1/2/45
    PHANTOM FORTUNE(E.S.Gardner)   1/3/50
    QUEENLY CONTESTANT(E.S.Gardner) 1/5/50
    RELUCTANT MODEL(E.S.Gardner)   1/1/37
    SHAPELY WIDOW(E.S.Gardner)   1/1/36
    SPURIOUS SPINSTER(E.S.Gardner)   1/1/36
    STEPDAUGHTER'S SECRET(E.S.Gardner) 1/2/45
    TROUBLED TRUSTEE(E.S.Gardner)   1/4/54
    WORRIED WAITRESS(E.S.Gardner)   1/4/54
R:THE CHINESE FIRE DRILL(M.Wolfe)   1/2/40
R:CLOAK AND DAGGER BIBLIOGRAPHY:AN ANNOTATED
  GUIDE TO SPY FICTION(M.J.Smith,Jr.)   1/4/50
R:DASHIELL HAMMETT:A DESCRIPTIVE BIBLIOGRAPHY
  (R.Layman)   3/6/49
R:DEAD LETTER(J.Valin)   5/6/46
R:THE DEAD SIDE OF THE MIKE(S.Brett)   5/2/28
R:DEADLY PATTERN(D.Clark)   3/3/46
R:DEATH AND THE GOOD LIFE((R.Hugo)   5/2/27
R:THE DETECTIVE IN HOLLYWOOD(J.Tuska)   2/4/38
R:DISCRETION(D.Linzee)   3/3/47
R:DOROTHY L.SAYERS:A LITERARY BIOGRAPHY(R.E.Hone) 3/5/45

M.Maarteens;Hammett;Chase;Review format   2/4/55
L:Authorship of Queen novels;M.Maartens;THE
    BLACK BOX MURDER   2/5/53
L:Wooster exists;Queen authorship;Charts   2/6/50
L:Response to Cox,Doran,Weber and Nevins;Loeser;
    Revealing endings;Favorite bookstore   3/4/54
L:Scholarship;Film column;French critical works;
    British reviews;Le Carre   5/5/46
R:THE ADVENTURES OF HERLOCK SHOLMES(P.Todd)   2/5/41
R:THE ADVENTURES OF JULES DE GRANDIN(S.Quinn)   1/2/42
R:ASIMOV'S SHERLOCKIAN LIMERICKS(I.Asimov)   2/4/42
R:THE CIRCULAR STAIRCASE(M.R.Rinehart)   1/5/38
R:A COFFIN FOR DIMITRIOS(E.Ambler)   2/4/39
R:THE COMPLETE UNCLE ABNER(M.D.Post)   2/5/9
R:THE COURTESY OF DEATH(G.Household)   4/3/45
R:THE CROOKED HINGE(J.D.Carr)   .   1/4/41
R:GREEN FOR DANGER(C.Brand)   2/6/38
R:THE IMPOSSIBLE VIRGIN(P.O'Donnell)   1/6/54
R:THE INTRIGUERS(D.Hamilton)   4/3/46
R:KEK HUUYGENS.SMUGGLER(R.L.Fish)   2/5/41
R:THE KING OF TERRORS(R.Bloch)   1/6/43
R:MURDER AT THE ABA(I.Asimov)   1/2/39
R:THE MYSTERY STORY(J.Ball.ed)   1/2/29
R:THE NEW SHOE(A.Upfield)   1/2/32
R:NIGHT SHIFT(S.King)   4/3/45
R:THE PIGEON PROJECT(I.Wallace)   3/3/44
R:RAFFLES OF THE ALBANY:FOOTSTEPS OF A FAMOUS
    GENTLEMAN CROOK IN THE TIMES OF THE GREAT
    DETECTIVE(B.Perowne)   4/3/44
R:SUCH STUFF AS SCREAMS ARE MADE OF(R.Bloch)   3/3/44
R:THE THEFTS OF NICK VELVET(E.D.Hoch)   2/6/39
R:THE THIRTEEN CRIMES OF SCIENCE FICTION
    (I.Asimov/M.H.Greenberg/C.Waugh,eds)   4/3/45
R:THE THIRTY-NINE STEPS(J.Buchan)   .   2/6/37
R:THE TRAGEDY OF X(E.Queen)   2/4/40
THE WRITER'S PROBE:RUTH RENDELL AS SOCIAL CRITIC
    (J.S.Bakerman)   3/5/3
Yates,Donald A.
    BOUCHERCON,1978:XI AND COUNTING   3/1/15
    FILM REVIEW:"Death On The Nile--Leisurely Peril"   3/1/45
    R:SEVEN SEATS TO THE MOON(C.Armstrong)   3/1/39
Young,Rachel   L:Mary Challis;Sara Woods   5/3/44

Mystery*File
Short Reviews by Steve Lewis

Joseph Hansen. *Gravedigger*. Holt, Rinehart & Winston, 1982, 183 pp., $12.50

There are certain key ingredients to a private eye story --a client with a tangled past, lots of clues, and a dogged determination to right wrongs. A certain folklore has developed, and each of these are part of it. If these are there, it doesn't matter what the hero of the tale really does for a living.

Take Dave Brandstetter, for example. He's been featured in five previous adventures before this one, and he works for an insurance company. His job is investigating death claims (the title of one of the earlier books in the series) and, on occasion, he solves murders before the police do.

He's assigned here to find a man who's made a claim on his missing daughter's policy but who in turn has just as mysteriously disappeared himself.

All the ingredients above are here. Working for himself, or working for a salary, whatever the tradition begun by Sam Spade and Philip Marlowe has become, Dave Brandstetter is certainly a part of it.

What makes him just a little bit different from all those other fictional detectives is that Dave Brandstetter is a homosexual, and his love affairs are just as much a part of the cases he solves as Mike Hammer's dames ever were.

In delicate, precise prose (considering, if you will, the genre in which he is writing), Hansen weaves in several subplots of man-sized proportions, some of which--it can't be denied--are of a highly personal nature.

These threads of the plot are also frank and unflinchingly honest. Brandstetter may not have all the answers to his life, but he reveals himself as a living, breathing person, who, more than most people, has a genuine awareness of who he really is. (B plus)* (*Reviews so marked have appeared earlier in the Hartford *Courant*.)

Jack Lynch. *Bragg's Hunch*. Fawcett Gold Medal, 1982, 189 pp., $2.25.

Whereas, on the other hand, Peter Bragg conforms almost exactly to the time-worn image everybody has of the tough, in-

dependent California private eye. Women appeal to him, of
course, but he doesn't knock himself out chasing them. Even
so (you guessed it), he still ends up with more of them on
this case than he knows what to do with.

   This is the first of a new series, based in San Francisco.
Bragg is hired by a self-made businessman* who needs protec-
tion. The man is especially worried that whoever is making
threats against him will start taking them out against his
young, teen-aged stepdaughter.

   The trail leads Bragg out to one of those legendary western whore-towns that exist maybe only in fiction. Before he's
hardly had time to turn around, or so it seems, he's managed
to set the two major criminal elements in town off one against
the other. A bloody gang war results, as fierce as anything
seen since Prohibition--or the days of Dashiell Hammett!

   All the right buttons are pressed. Somehow the right
spark refuses to go off. Some well-drawn touches show some
insight into character--some blatant, some subtle--but for the
most part, well, let's just say the action peaks too soon.
(B minus)

Thomas B. Dewey. *Can a Mermaid Kill?* Tower, 1965, 189 pp.

   Yes. (C plus)

Joyce Harrington. *Family Reunion*. St. Martin's, 1982, 304
   pp., $13.95.

   To quote one of the leading characters halfway through
this long, sinister, psychological melodrama, there are some
families that should stay as far apart from each other as pos-
sible, and Jenny Holland's is one of them.

   Seized by a fit of Ray Bradburyian nostalgia, Jenny returns
to her small midwestern home town hoping to make amends with
her estranged mother. Quicker than she realizes, she ends up
learning more about her immediate family that she ever really
wanted to know.

   In a way strikingly akin to the standard tradition built
up by today's cinema of the macabre, the various relatives
gathered together find themselves huddled up like sheep against
each other, with someone--or something--fiercely nipping at
their flanks.

   Harrington's approach is literate and subtle, however, and
the copious amounts of blood, gore, and gloriously bizarre
deaths are left (thankfully) to what was once affectionately
known as the silver screen.

   Nevertheless--and it goes almost without saying--all of
the characters involved are either naive, neurotic, or merely
bewildered in one way or another.

   If this were not s,o, the obvious solution would be for
everyone to vacate the premises at once. Of course, for the
sake of the book, they do not.

   For anyone with more than a smidgeon of imagination, a
reasonable explanation for what's going on will assert itself

------

   *Which, of course, is a polite way of saying he has a finger
in a good many sleaze-joints around the Bay area.

at once. This solves about half the puzzle. The other half of the answer will make your flesh creep, and there will be little warning. What makes this all the more remarkable is that none of this has anything to do with ghosts, the spirit world, or the supernatural. Harrington, an Edgar-winning short-story writer, is content to work with the normal aberrations of human nature. In itself alone, this is more than enough to double the impact of the final secret of Jenny's mother. (B plus)*

Dick Francis. *Twice Shy*. Putnam's, 1982, 307 pp., $13.95.

Over the years Dick Francis has become a very good writer. He's always been an exceptional story-teller. Ever since he turned to writing mysteries, at the end of his career as a well-known steeple-chase jockey, his strength has been the inside knowledge he has of the world of championship racing. In one way or another, he's displayed it to good advantage in every one of his books, all of them involving horses.

Studying and absorbing a collection of the complete Dick Francis, over twenty volumes at present count, would constitute a sure-fire education in picking and producing the next Derby winner, redeemable at any track in the United Kingdom. Thrown in at no extra charge would be a full blow-by-blow description of all the pitfalls the unwary horseman may encounter along the way.

Horses are in Dick Francis' blood, and in that of every one of his heroes. It is also contagious. Even confirmed city-dwellers who have ridden a horse but once--like myself, or was it that the horse condescended to let me ride him?--or those who abominate all horsey stories from *Black Beauty* on up will find themselves caught up in the excitement and the mystique and the thrill of the pounding final stretch. And that's no mean accomplishment!

In *Twice Shy* we get two stories for the price of one. A pair of brothers, both innocent victims, find themselves threatened in turn by one of Francis' patented and typically brutal villains--one in the first half, the other in the second.

Angelo Gilbert is certainly as bloodthirsty and despicably cruel an opponent as we've come to expect, but he's also far less clever, and he proves much less of a challenge to be disposed of than that faced by most of Francis' heroes. The fray is not without casualties--don't be mistaken--but in spite of the tenseness of the various situations brothers Jonathan and William Derry unwittingly find themselves in, neither seems as overly taxed as they might have been.

At stake is a computerized betting system that, if it really existed, would be worth millions. For the most part, however, keep in mind that gambling is strictly a mugs' game. William Derry's book-making friend Taff is a fine example. Gambling is a way of life in which only the good mathematicians survive. As far as a successful system for betting on the horses is concerned, well, if anyone has one, and it works, it's like the perfect crime--nobody's telling anybody else about it.

From off-the-cuff handicapping, to the expertise of modern-day computer technology, Dick Francis' name under the title of

the book still means there's plenty of excitement in store,
from start to finish. This outing's certainly no exception,
but all in all I think Francis was coasting more than he
usually does. (B plus)*

Clive Cussler. *Night Probe*. Bantam, 1982, 345 pp., $3.95.

After helping raise the Titanic last time out, what could
there possibly be for Dirk Pitt to do for an encore? As
America's number one underwater super-agent, even he would
seem hard pressed to come up with something to top that one.
The year is 1989, far enough into tht future for the
United States to be realistically sinking slowly into bank-
ruptcy, desperately in need of new sources of energy, and yet
near enough to avoid being passed off as mere science·fiction.
Missing are two vitally needed copies of a treaty made
with England in 1914, one that would have sold Canada to the
United States to help finance the early stages of World War I,
but lost to the pages of history by an amazing series of
tragic accidents.
One copy is in an ocean liner now residing at the bottom
of the St. Lawrence Seaway. The other is somewhere on a train
which met its doom on the very same day, crashing through a
bridge crossing the Hudson River.
Together, their twin disappearances mark one of the great-
est vanishing acts of all time. (The treaty was secret. Why
is it that hardly anybody remembers either disaster?) The
President puts all his faith in Dirk Pitt to produce another
miracle.
Not to be caught napping, Britain calls out of retirement
one of the most famous spies the world has ever known, just
for the occasion. He is known as "Brian Shaw" in this book,
but that won't fool any of his many fans for·a minute. Reknown
as both a ladies' man and for his even more famous license to
kill, "Shaw" proves he has lost none of·his touch for either.
In a word, Clive Cussler's technical expertise in matters
aquanautical is impressive, but if anything his knack for
telling a spell-binder of a story is even more so. Like the
old penny-a-word pulpsters, or the directors of the great
adventure serials of yesteryear, Cussler is a master of action,
intrigue, and romance (not necessarily in that order), and the
pace is never allowed to slacken for a moment.
If you missed the hardcover, also by Bantam (1981), the
paperback is now out. You could wait for the movie, I suppose,
but why? (A)

Steven Frimmer. *Dead Matter*. Holt, Rinehart & Winston, 1982,
220 pp., $13.50.

The beginning writer is often admonished to "write what
you know," sometimes over and over again. Steven Frimmer is
an editor at a New York publishing house, and he's probably
had occasion to give this same advice to a good many fledgling
authors over the years--and all of them more or less receptive,
I'm sure!
But if it's so, he certainly practices what he preaches,
as he most capably demonstrates here.

This is Frimmer's first venture into mystery fiction. Involved is a senior editor at a small New York publishing house
(surprise!) and lots of dastardly doings in the world of books:
in-fighting, back-stabbing, and love-making, plus a totally
unexpected spy trip to Istanbul, courtesy of the CIA.
All the makings, in fact, of a truly funny and engaging
little thriller.
Back in New York a murder is also committed, and a new
detective emerges on the scene: British personality-host
Hartley Dobbs--sort of a David Frost with an affinity for
crime.
For those who pride themselves on their armchair detecting
ability, too much of what happens is forced to take place off-
stage, and the reader is left to learn about it too late to do
any good.
The fascinating world of editing and publishing offers
more than mere background, however. Tied up and neatly inte-
grated into both the crime and its solution is the psychology
of the people who work with books--the way they think. It's a
plus, and it's nicely done. (B)*

Roy Harley Lewis. *A Cracking of Spines*. St. Martin's, 1981,
    207 pp., $10.95.

Mood, atmosphere, and background are essential attributes
of a detective story, but in and of themselves they're hardly
enough.
Any number of examples abound, but let's take *A Cracking
of Spines* as one in particular. Mystery readers invariably
gobble up mysteries that involve both books and book collec-
tors, so at first glance here's one that would go right away.
Completely permeating Matthew Coll's hunt for a ruthless
gang of antiquarian book thieves is a love for the printed
page and showy leather bindings, but--and it hurts to say this
--that's about all this book has going for it. The plot has
to be turned upside down before it begins to make any sense at
all.
Coll, formerly of military intelligence, is now retired as
--guess what?--the new owner of a small English bookshop. His
detective abilities turn out to be hampered by a puzzling
taste in women, however, and he cripples his own investigation
by two disastrous (and obvious) errors in judgment.
In spite of his several faults as a detective, Coll is a
rather likeable fellow, and I'll be looking forward to his
follow-up case, due to be published any day now. Let's hope
it's a little bit more solid than this one, though. (C)*

Verdicts
More Reviews

Nicholas Freeling. *Wolfnight*. Heinemann, 1982, 200 pp.

The back dust-jacket flap of Nicholas Freeling's latest
novel notes that Freeling's current home, near Strasbourg,
"once farm, bakery, country pub, is now a lighthouse on a twi-
lit Europe." This statement may indicate that for once the
writer of the blurb has actually read some Freeling and has
probably read this book. For in *Wolfnight* Freeling sets the
tone through one of the protagonist's early musings:

> Twilight made things sinister. Why else is the moment before
> darkness falls called "entre chein et loup"? Between dog and
> wolf ... when, conceivably, the werewolf could still present a
> blameless air of domesticity. (p. 3)

Once again, Henri Castang, Richard (his superior in the
police force), and Orthez (an unlikely but effective right-
hand man) confront evil in the shape of murder and political
intrigue. The suspicious death of the mistress of a government
official draws these familiar officers of France's Police
Judiciaire into an intrigue which could not only ruin their
careers but also bring them sudden, probably unavenged, death.
In effect, in seeking justice--and, here, in trying to stave
off political upheaval--these three representatives of whatever order and decency is (in Freeling's view) left in the
western world wage a dangerous, lonely battle against money,
power, ambition, and misled but sometimes sincere dedication
to another political order.
Regular readers of Castang's novels will know that honor
and decency alone are ample motivation for the Castang group
to undertake this mission, but in *Wolfnight* they are further
spurred by the kidnapping of Vera Castang, an event which also
threatens the couple's infant daughter. Certainly, the evil
doers will stop at nothing; that is made clear. What is
equally clear and perhaps even more frightening is the fact
that Castang and Richard must move outside the law in order
to uphold it, serve justice, and maintain order. Yet, who
would have it otherwise? And with this question, Freeling
closes the novel, leaving the reader to ask (as always) where
does society go from here?
Perhaps no other crime writer practicing today is so
adroit at combining action with philosophical and political

46

speculation. Perhaps no crime writer practicing today is capable of so broadly based, so competent use of allusion; literature, music, art, television--all provide shadings of tone and character which serve to inform and remind every reader that no Castang adventure is simply the story of one crime, but is rather the story of the many crimes which strike at the heart of the western cultural and political heritage. Further, Castang, Vera, and Richard are full, complex characters who remain interesting because they grow and develop--and, in Richard's case, have rich, sometimes murky backgrounds which are slowly revealed. Additionally, stunning new characters are presented, particularly Madame Alberthe de Rubempré, one of Freeling's attractive destructors, and no one creates such creatures better than he. All in all, then, *Wolfnight* is strong stuff, a novel which does its series and its author proud. (Jane S. Bakerman)

J.C. Pollock. *Mission M.I.A.* Crown, 1982, 274 pp., $12.95.

J.C. Pollock's first novel capitalizes on without exploiting the recent publicity about the more than 2,500 U.S. servicemen still listed as missing in action after the Vietnam War. It was written with the technical assistance of several U.S. Army Speical Forces personnel and has been praised for its verisimilitude by certain elements of the military community.
The plot is simple. Frank Detimore, after eleven brutal years as a P.O.W. in the jungles of Vietnam, manages to smuggle a letter to his wife, Betty. She goes to the Department of Defense expecting assistance, but they call the letter a forgery and shrug her off. Disappointed but determined, Betty turns to Jack Callahan, one of Detimore's former Green Beret comrades, and convinces him to organize a mission to rescue Detimore. With the aid of Betty's father's money, Callahan looks up the four other former members of Detimore's squad, supervises a week of training, obtains weapons and supplies, and plans a difficult, dangerous rescue mission. Of course there are unforeseen complications which make the mission even more hazardous than was planned.
In his stark, straightforward style, Pollock describes the horrors of the P.O.W. camps, the danger of relying on unprincipled mercenaries, and the relationship between the Special Forces and the Montagnard natives. But he is at his most effective when describing military actions and situations that are well suited for generating suspense. Callahan's team must make a very difficult night-time HALO (High Altitude-Low Opening) parachute jump into the jungle; later, Callahan must silently "disable" the sentry guards at the P.O.W. camp before the team enters. There is the constant danger of being discovered and captured by a company of North Vietnamese soldiers at a nearby army base. There are bureaucratic stratagems and hints of double cross.
Pollock knows the modern military mind quite well. Callahan and his teammates do not believe in the old-fashioned concept of heroism ("I'd die for my country") but in their pragmatic way still find room for plenty of courage. This might seem to be more of a war novel than a suspense novel, but it is quite similar to many of the spy stories of the fifties and sixties in which the agent's mission was to penetrate the ham-

boo or iron curtain on a rescue mission. *Mission M.I.A.* will probably be regarded and remembered more for its timeliness and realism than for novelistic merits, but I found it suspenseful and at times gripping. (Greg Goode)

David Carkeet. *Double Negative.* Penguin, 1982 (first published by Dial Press in 1980), 246 pp., $2.95.

Highly praised by Newgate Callendar and others for its originality, *Double Negative* is the story of the murder of one of the staff linguists at the Wabash Institute in Indiana. The linguists there study language development in children, and when one of these professionals is found dead in the office chair of Jeremy Cook, the Institute's most famous scholar, their peaceful, almost soporific daily routine is disrupted. The body in Cook's chair, along with a dent in the hood of Cook's car matching the shape of the victim's head, make Cook the prime suspect. Although there is a small-town police detective, Lieutenant Leaf, on hand, his investigation tends to incriminate Crook, so Cook must detect for himself. The other suspects are a motley bunch of idiosyncratic linguist-scholar-researchers: Cook's friend Woeps, with his perennial bad luck; nosy, gossipy Aaskhugh, the oneupsman; Milke, the bearded lady-killer; the mysterious, ever-laughing Orffman; and the scholar-turned-administrator Wach, the head of the Institute.
    Alongside the detection plot there is a subplot which is given so much space that we know it will become relevant to the detection. Cook is studying ideophenomena in children, and is trying to interpret the meaning of "m-bwee," a disyllabic utterance repeated over and over by Woeps' sixteen-month-old son. Cook succeeds as the crime is solved.
    The characters are all well drawn and interesting. The dialogue varies in texture. Of special delight is the dialogue between the fat, puffing, vulgar, funny, beef-and-burgundy complexioned Lieutenant Leaf and the sensitive, intellectual Cook. Author Carkeet, as an English Professor at the University of Missouri, is perhaps well qualified to sketch the various profiles of *homo Thinktankicus.* Through the professional trials and tribulations of Cook and his colleagues, Carkeet gives us an insider's view of the fantasies and defense mechanisms of the stereotypical intellectual--but all served up with generous dashes of humor.
    Comparisons with Golden Age classical detective stories have been given and are apt. There are "double negative" metaphors scattered throughout as red herrings, and even several charts which aid the detection. Perhaps because I had read several reviews before I read the book itself, I was expecting to be much more dazzled than I was at the coming together of the two plot strands and at logical and linguistic fireworks. I was able to infer the method of solution, but not the identity of the murderer., It was well worth the time, and I am looking forward to Carkeet's next book. (Greg Goode)

John R. Feegel. *The Dance Card.* Avon, 1982 (first published by Dial Press in 1981), 312 pp., $2.95.

Like Feegel's two previous books, *Death Sails the Bay* and

the Edgar-winning *Autopsy, The Dance Card* has a pathologist as
the hero. The book is a fairly well crafted combination of
military inverted crime story and *roman à clef*.

Atlanta Police Department's Medical Examiner is pathologist
Twig Stanton, who is called to the luxurious Hyatt Regency
Hotel to scoop up and examine a "jumper," an apparent suicide
who had jumped off the twenty-sixth floor balcony. Stanton
soon discovers that the person had not jumped, that he was a
Navy pathologist, and that several people had been after the
Navy man looking for something they thought he had. Stanton
also discovers the dance card.

The middle two-thirds of the book contains the story of
the Navy pathologist, George Toll. Toll is sent by the Navy
and the CIA to a government installation on Key West in 1961,
right as the Bay of Pigs attack was bieng planned. Toll is
given an assignment which is mysterious, top secret, and very
unethical. He keeps a record of his activities, which he
calls a "dance card," and later, after the mission, writes to
the CIA to tell them this fact. After the CIA learns of Toll's
record we see them hounding and persecuting him for the next
twenty years to recover it. From a Navy base at Bethesda,
Maryland, to a lonely assignment on Midway Island, from the
primitive hills of Hispaniola to posh Atlanta, Toll goes on
his Candide-like string of assignments, trying to keep the CIA
from finding the dance card.

The two plots, Toll's and Stanton's, come logically but
abruptly together on Stanton's autopsy table, as he finds
Toll's dance card hidden behind a false appendectomy scar.
(This sounds like a giveaway of sorts, but the book's back
cover tells as much.) Now it is Stanton's job to decide what
the dance card means and what to do about it, because the CIA
soon discovers that he has it.

What is special about *The Dance Card* is that, unlike many
espionage stories that contain horrendous government cover-ups
discovered only *after* the fact, it gives an inverted view of
what is later covered up. The dialogue is a bit flat, all the
characters talk somewhat alike, and there are several gram-
matical errors, but these are the only weaknesses in an otherwise suspenseful book. (Greg Goode)

Lucille Kallen. *C.B. Greenfield: No Lady in the House*. Wynd-
   ham Books, 1982, 224 pp., $13.50.

C.B. Greenfield and his engaging associate Maggie Rome
make their third appearance in this, the strongest of the
Greenfield series to date. When a domestic is murdered in
Charlie Greenfield's house, he vows to find the murderer,
pulling along a reluctant and mystified Maggie. Before we get
to the end of the trail, we've followed Maggie and her boss to
Florida and through the convolutions of politics in Sloan's
Ford, the rural town in New York where Greenfield publishes a
weekly newspaper.

As with the earlier stories, Maggie does the legwork while
Greenfield mysteriously pieces together the puzzle of murder
and burglary.

Also as usual, Kallen holds back the clues enabling Greenfield to arrive at the truth before the reader. It's a bit
trying, perhaps, but Kallen more than makes up for this with

the style and wit used in the further delineation of her principal characters. All in all, *No Lady in the House* is entertaining and readable. (Alan S. Mosier)

Betty Suyker. *Death Scene*. St. Martin's Press, 1981, 220
pp., $10.95.

Molly McConnell is a researcher for a news magazine.
That's all she does. Her life is her job. In her head are
all kinds of facts. She'd be great at trivia, but then I
guess that goes with the job.
Molly meets Mike Brennan and together they get involved in
a murder on the Great White Way, Broadway. How they manage to
solve the mystery is quite entertaining. Betty Suyker spices
up the plot with lots of color. She has the requisite number
of stereotyped actors and actresses for a mostly humorous investigation.
After a slow start, *Death Scene* takes off at a fast pace.
This is not so much a murder mystery--although a suitable
theatrical murder occurs--as it is an exercise in deductive
reasoning. *Why* elderly actress Isobel St. George was murdered is far more interesting than the eventual discovery of
who the murderer is.
Without giving away the nicely constructed plot, let me
only say "Brush up your Shakespeare." Knowledge of the bard's
works will prove the solution to the crime and the mystery.
(Alan S. Mosier)

Lawrence Treat. *Crime and Puzzlement*. David R. Godine, 1981,
69 pp., $4.95.

The subtitle is "24 solve-them-yourself picture mysteries."
My favorite parts are the thirties-style cover and Treat's entertaining introduction regarding how he came to write the
book.
Each mystery consists of a scene-of-the-crime picture, a
brief description of the crime, and several questions about
it. Solutions are in the back of the book. None of the puzzles are very hard, but they are entertaining enough to keep
your interest. A great gift! (Linda Toole)

Tim Heald. *Unbecoming Habits*. Hutchinson, 1973.

The first case recorded of low-key government agent
(small, rather obscure department) Simon Bognor. The setting
is an old priory and the victims come from within the ranks of
the inmates. So the question is, what on earth could there be
in a priory to warrant such blood-letting? Bognor eventually
finds out. Reasonable detection. Some mild humor. Promising, without rising to any great heights. Recently televised
over here as part of a Bognor series. (Bob Adey)

www.ingramcontent.com/pod-product-compliance
Lightning Source LLC
Chambersburg PA
CBHW031616040426
42452CB00006B/545